YOU CAN DRAW FANTASY FIGURES
DRAWING HEROIC WARRIORS

BY STEVE SIMS

Gareth Stevens
Publishing

Please visit our Web site, www.garethstevens.com. For a free color catalog of all our high-quality books, call toll free 1-800-542-2595 or fax 1-877-542-2596.

Library of Congress Cataloging-in-Publication Data

Sims, Steve (Steve P.), 1980-
Drawing heroic warriors / Steve Sims.
    p. cm. – (You can draw fantasy figures)
Includes bibliographical references and index.
ISBN 978-1-4339-4052-1 (library binding)
ISBN 978-1-4339-4053-8 (pbk.)
ISBN 978-1-4339-4054-5 (6-pack)
1. Heroes in art–Juvenile literature. 2. Fantasy in art–
Juvenile literature. 3. Drawing–Technique–Juvenile literature.
I. Title.
NC825.H45S56 2011
743.4–dc22

                            2010013016

First Edition

Published in 2011 by
Gareth Stevens Publishing
111 East 14th Street, Suite 349
New York, NY 10003

Copyright © 2011 Arcturus Publishing

Artwork and Text: Steve Sims
Editors: Kate Overy and Joe Harris
Designer: Steve Flight

Printed in the United States of America

CPSIA compliance information: Batch #AS10GS: For further information contact Gareth Stevens, New York, New York at
1-800-542-2595.

SL001641US

CONTENTS

Drawing and Inking Tips

In the world of swords and sorcery, heroes can perform extraordinary feats of valor that would be impossible in the real world. However, it's still essential that your characters should look solid and believable. So here are some helpful hints to keep in mind.

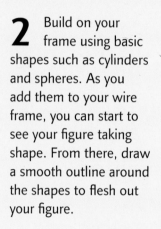

1 First, work out your hero's posture and attitude using a wire frame. You can look in the mirror to work out how a pose might work!

2 Build on your frame using basic shapes such as cylinders and spheres. As you add them to your wire frame, you can start to see your figure taking shape. From there, draw a smooth outline around the shapes to flesh out your figure.

HUMAN HEIGHT = 7 HEADS

TOP TIP!

Most adult human figures are seven times the height of their head. Draw your character's head, then calculate his or her height by measuring three heads for the legs, one for the lower torso, and two for the upper body.

3 When things are looking good and your character is complete, you can start to ink the picture. Inking allows us to choose the best lines we have drawn in pencil and make them stand out from the rest.

Coloring Tips

1 After the inking stage, it's time to color your characters. Plan your color scheme, then start laying down your base tones.

2 Next, color your shaded areas using darker tones of the base colors. Note the shadows on our warrior's arms, face, and hair.

3 Finally, add some highlights to areas where light would reflect, using whites and lighter shades. Note how this brings a shine to the metal blade of this axe.

MALE WARRIOR

This highly trained warrior is a fearless protector of the lands of light, and fights with unrivaled fury to uphold all that is good. All weapons are deadly in his hands, and all opponents shall fall at his feet.

1 Start by drawing your basic frame. The male warrior is ready to attack in this aggressive action pose.

2 Warriors are tough fighting machines with broad shoulders and muscular legs, so build on your wire frame with some hefty blocks as a base for all those muscles.

3 Once you have all of your basic shapes in place, draw around them to give your figure a smooth outline. At this point, you can erase your wire frame. Pencil in your warrior's hair and the shape of his sword.

4 When you're happy with the outline of your figure, erase all of your basic shapes so that you have a clean pencil drawing. Now you can start adding detail. Pencil in your warrior's clothing, leather arm cuffs, shield, and dagger. Give him a determined battle-ready expression, furrowed brow, and an open, yelling mouth that will strike fear into the hearts of all who stand in his way!

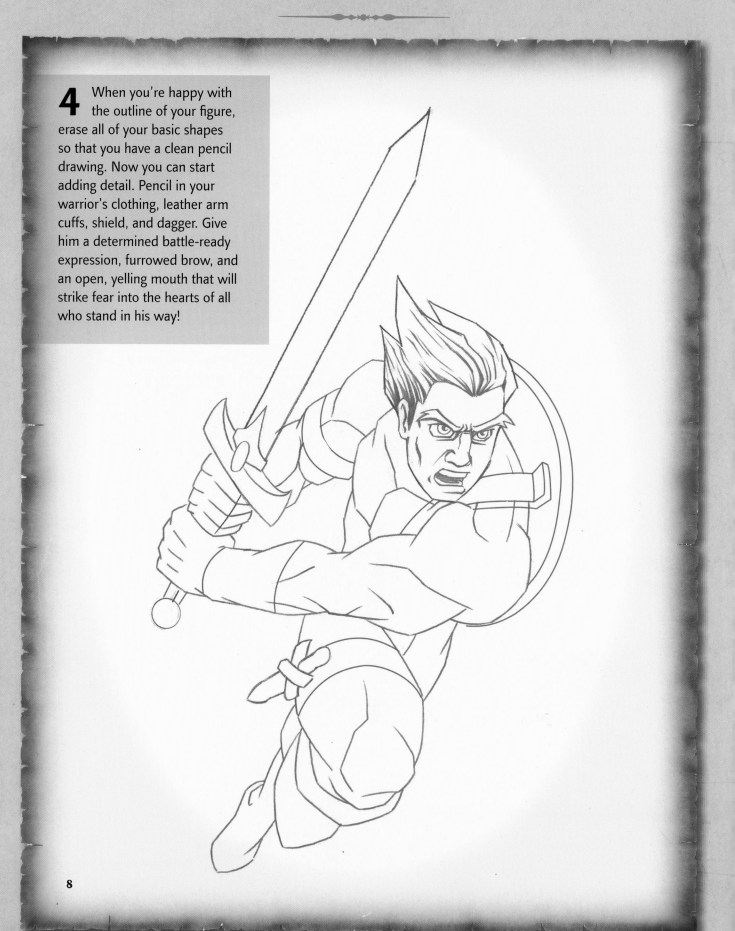

5 This is your final pencil stage, so it's time to add all of the fine details. Notice the worn look of his wooden shield, the detail on his weapons, and the muscle tone of his skin. Before you ink your character, plan the areas where light hits your figure, and add shading to places that are in shadow.

TOP TIP !

To make your warrior look really battle-hardened, add a few scars and wounds from previous battles.

9

6 Now ink your character, going over your best pencil lines. Add darker, solid ink to the areas that are in shadow, which will add depth to your figure.

7 The final step is to color your warrior. Try to use shades that will enhance the different textures in the image. Use a bright yellow-gold for his metal sword, and muted browns for his wooden shield and leather boots. Use white to highlight where the light shines on his shield and the areas where it hits his body.

FEMALE WARRIOR

Loyal to her king, this agile fighter
charges into battle with the ferocity
and heart of a warrior twice her size,
fighting for the forces of good. Many
have judged her by her size,
and many have not lived to
do so again.

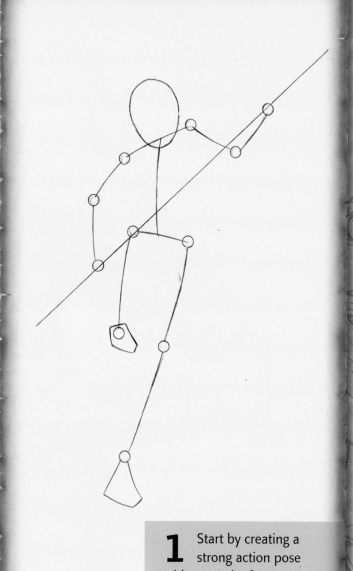

1 Start by creating a
strong action pose
with your wire frame.
The female warrior's
body is angled to the side
of her leading leg, while
her other leg is bent up
behind her as she runs.

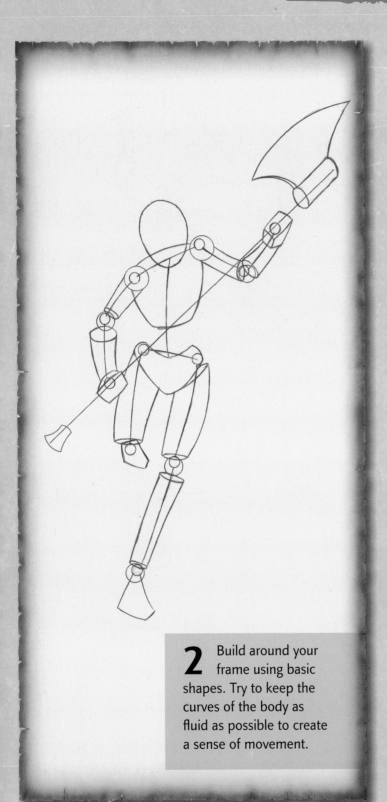

2 Build around your frame using basic shapes. Try to keep the curves of the body as fluid as possible to create a sense of movement.

3 Once you can see your figure taking shape, remove your wire frame and draw around the shapes to create your outline. Start to add her clothing and hair.

4 Erase all of your basic shapes so that you're left with a clean pencil outline, then start adding detail. Give her some body armor and finalize her clothing, adding a cloak and boots. Give her expression as much attitude as you would a male warrior, but draw almond-shaped eyes, a smaller nose, and hopefully less stubble!

5 Now add the fine detail to your warrior woman. Think about the folds and creases in the fabric of her cloak and add shading to show its depth. Give her body armor a chain mail look in contrast to the soft fur trim around her cloak and boots.

TOP TIP !

If your character is running toward the viewer, don't forget to have their hair flowing behind them to heighten the sense of movement and direction.

6 When inking your character, try to keep as many of the fine, detailed lines from your final pencil drawing as you can. Use heavier lines to define muscle tone, and solid areas of black ink to add depth.

7 Now it's time to color your character. Keeping your color palette simple and adding flashes of bright colors can be very effective. Shades of gray work well for her armor and weapon. Remember to add highlights to give the metal a reflective quality.

DWARF WARRIOR

From the stone kingdom of the Western Mountains comes this mighty warrior. Armed with incredible strength and determination, this dwarf likes nothing more than seeing evil fall beneath the power of his ancient hammer.

1 Start by drawing the basic stick figure. The dwarf warrior's body is short and stocky, and he is ready for battle.

2 Dwarves are sturdy and tough, with broad shoulders and muscular legs, so build on your wire frame with some hefty blocks as a base for all of those muscles.

3 Keep building on your figure, removing your stick figure lines as it takes shape. The dome of his head will form the basis for his helmet. Add the horns on either side. Pencil in his beard, clothing, boots, and armor. Flesh out his hands and arms, and use blocks to divide his hammer's head into sections.

19

4 Finalize your pencil drawing, erasing your construction shapes as you go along. You now have the basis of a pretty dangerous warrior. Start adding the finishing touches, like all the creases in his clothing and the detail on his helmet. Give him a determined, battle-ready expression.

5 Clean up the lines you have drawn, then add in all of your final detail and shading. This will really bring your dwarf warrior to life.

TOP TIP !

Small details such as chips and cracks will help to make a weapon look old and battle-worn.

6 Now you have everything in place—it's time to ink over your final pencil lines. Try to keep lots of the fine detail, like the chips and battle damage to his weapon and armor plating.

7 The final step is to color your warrior, which will really bring him to life. He is a brave and strong character, so rich colors will add a sense of heroism to his outfit. Give him a white beard and don't forget to add highlights to the metal of his armor.

The Battlefield

Now that you've mastered how to draw three different types of characters, it's time to create a setting in which our heroes can appear. So welcome to the scene outside Blood Keep, a fortress our valiant champions must protect at all costs.

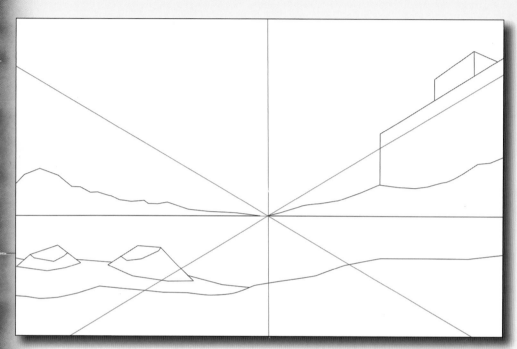

1 In this scene we have a central vanishing point, with perspective lines radiating from it. Elements such as the castle walls will follow the perspective lines until they hit that spot. Use the lines to plot out the basic shapes of the landscape and castle.

2 Next, add some extra elements and foreground detail, concentrating on simple shapes. Sketch out some pennants and battlements for the fortress; banners and weapons of fallen warriors on the battlefield; and some sinister skulls. You can put in as many elements as you like, depending on how busy you want your scene to be.

CREATING A SCENE

3 Flesh out your picture with more details, such as the tattered edges on the war banner and eye sockets on the skulls. Don't worry, you don't need to draw in every blade of grass! Concentrate on a few areas, including the foreground, and it will give the impression that the entire area is grass-covered.

4 Your completed pencil drawing should look something like this. Finish off by adding fine details, such as the texture of the rocks, skulls, and wooden poles, and the brickwork of the castle. Think about where shadows would be cast, and add shading. Remember to clean up any unwanted lines.

5 Now add some ink to your image. Remember to use dark, heavy inking in the foreground, and finer, lighter lines as objects get further away. This will help to give the image depth.

6 The colors you choose for your scene will dictate its atmosphere. Dark, nighttime colors will create a sense of foreboding, while bright, daytime colors will create a sense of hope and optimism. A colorful sunset or sunrise—like the one shown here—suggests that things are about to change. But will they change for better or worse?

Movement and Combat

Once you are more confident with the basic construction of human-like characters, you can start experimenting with the way figures move. Try putting them in different action poses with different props and weapons.

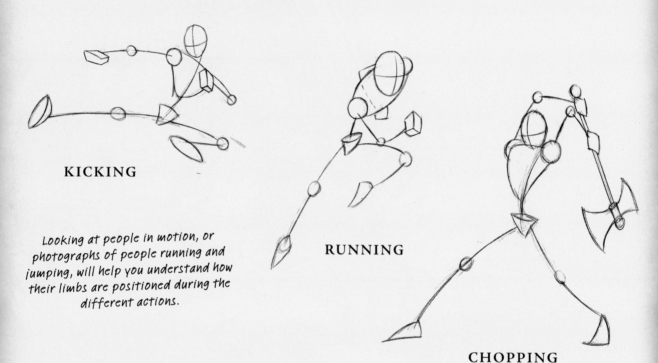

KICKING

Looking at people in motion, or photographs of people running and jumping, will help you understand how their limbs are positioned during the different actions.

RUNNING

CHOPPING

Drawing two characters fighting isn't as hard as it might seem at first.
Follow the same steps that you would to create one character, but do it with two!

1 Draw the basic frame of one character first, and then the frame of his or her opponent. Build on the frames using your basic shapes, remembering how perspective will work on your characters, and that their sizes might differ depending on what sort of creature they are.

30

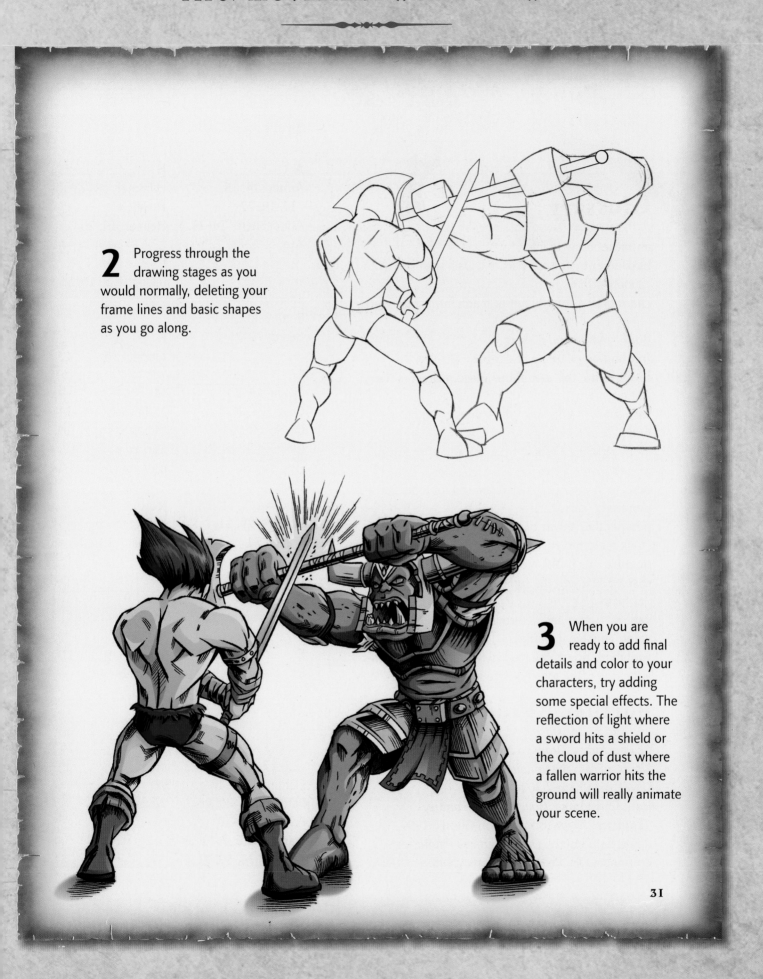

2 Progress through the drawing stages as you would normally, deleting your frame lines and basic shapes as you go along.

3 When you are ready to add final details and color to your characters, try adding some special effects. The reflection of light where a sword hits a shield or the cloud of dust where a fallen warrior hits the ground will really animate your scene.

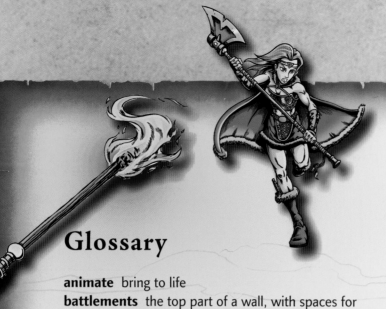

Glossary

animate bring to life

battlements the top part of a wall, with spaces for shooting through

chain mail a kind of armor made from small metal rings linked together

fluid smooth and flowing

foreboding warning of danger

foreground the part of the image nearest to the viewer

furrowed marked with deep lines or wrinkles

hefty heavy and large

highlights the lightest colored parts of an image

muted soft and calm

palette the range of colors chosen for a picture

pennants narrow flags

perspective a way of drawing that makes objects look three-dimensional

posture the position of someone's body

texture the way the surface of an object looks or feels

valiant brave and determined

valor courage in battle

vanishing point the place where perspective lines appear to come together into a point

Further Reading

Cowan, Finlay. *Drawing and Painting Fantasy Figures: From the Imagination to the Page*. London: David and Charles, 2004.

Hart, Christopher. *How to Draw Fantasy Characters*. New York: Watson-Guptill, 1999.

Renaigle, Damon J. *Draw Medieval Fantasies*. Cincinnati, OH: Peel Productions, 1995.

Index